My First Book of

SHAPES and NUMBERS

KIRAN REKHA BANERJI

RED TURTLE
RUPA

Published in Red Turtle by
Rupa Publications India Pvt. Ltd 2017
7/16, Ansari Road, Daryaganj
New Delhi 110002

Sales centres:
Allahabad Bengaluru Chennai
Hyderabad Jaipur Kathmandu
Kolkata Mumbai

Text Copyright © Kiran Rekha Banerji 2017
Illustrations Copyright © Rupa Publications India Pvt. Ltd 2017
Design by Roy Creation

The views and opinions expressed in this book are the author's own and the facts are as reported by him/her which have been verified to the extent possible, and the publishers are not in any way liable for the same.

All rights reserved.
No part of this publication may be reproduced, transmitted,
or stored in a retrieval system, in any form or by any means,
electronic, mechanical, photocopying, recording or otherwise,
without the prior permission of the publisher.

ISBN: 978-81-291-4556-7

First impression 2017

10 9 8 7 6 5 4 3 2 1

The moral right of the author has been asserted.

Printed at Shree Maitrey Printech Pvt. Ltd, Noida

This book is sold subject to the condition that it shall not,
by way of trade or otherwise, be lent, resold, hired out,
or otherwise circulated, without the publisher's prior consent,
in any form of binding or cover other than that
in which it is published.

This book belongs to:

....
....

TRIANGLE

A TRIANGLE can be made by joining three straight lines. It has three corners. When you draw a mountain it will have the shape of a triangle. Let us fix a tent for you to play. It also looks like a triangle from the front and the back.

How many triangle shapes can you find in the picture?

ACT : Take some small straws and place them to make a triangle. Help the child to make the same.

SQUARE

Pick up a dice. All its sides are of the same size. This shape is called a SQUARE. It has four corners. You can turn it any way you want but it always looks the same. You need four straws to make a square. Some of the building blocks in your toy set are square.

ACT : Spread a napkin and see the shape that it forms. Is it a square? Fold it twice to get a square.

RECTANGLE

You sometimes get presents in a box that has two big and two small sides. It has four corners too. This shape is a RECTANGLE. If you take two big and two small straws you can make a rectangle. Most of your books and chocolates are rectangles too.

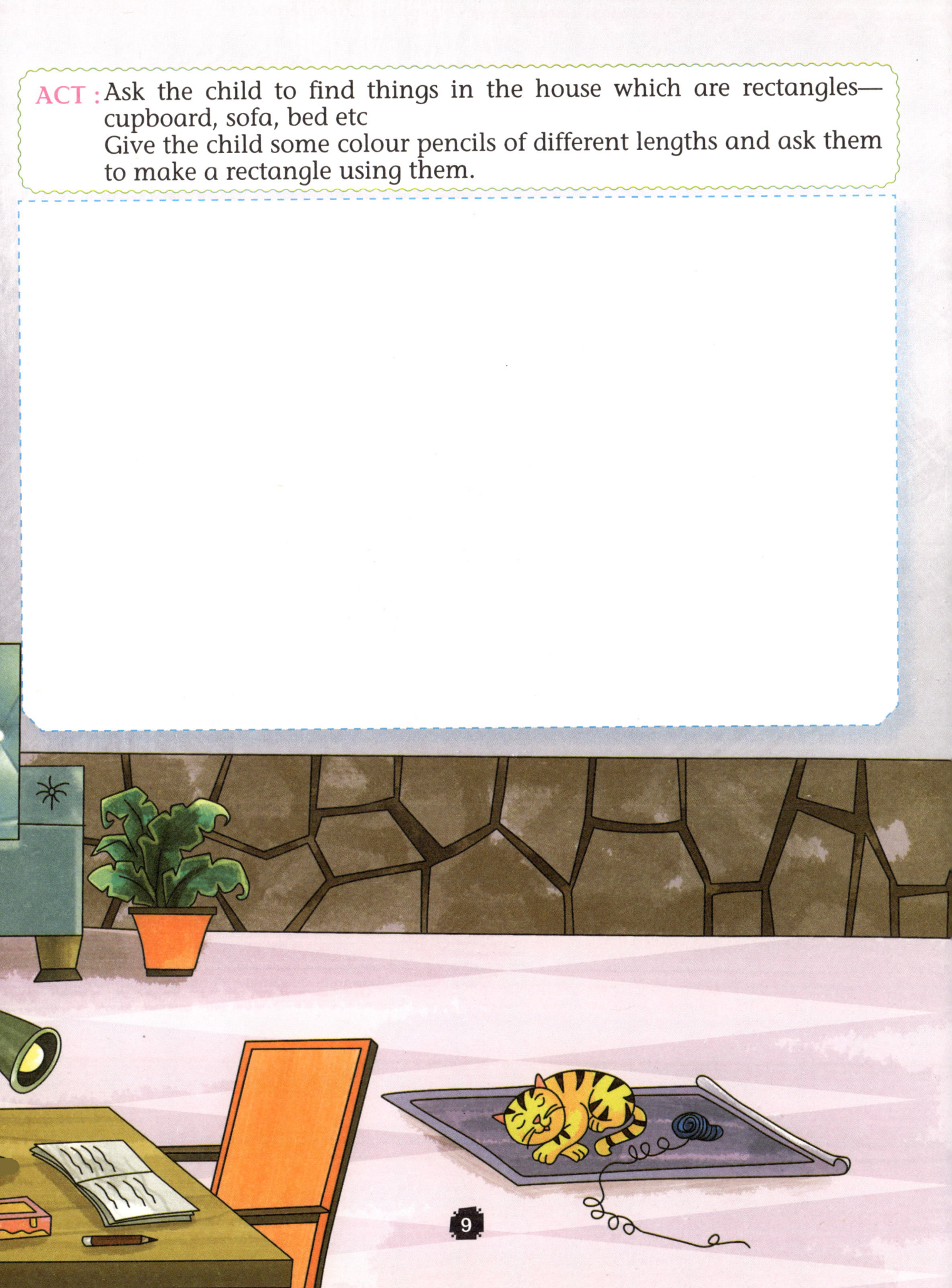

ACT : Ask the child to find things in the house which are rectangles—cupboard, sofa, bed etc
Give the child some colour pencils of different lengths and ask them to make a rectangle using them.

CIRCLE

Look at the ball you have. It is round in shape. You can also draw a ball on a piece of paper. This shape is a CIRCLE. A circle has no corner. Some of your toys are in the shape of a circle too. The full moon is a big circle in the sky. Your favourite smilies are also circles.

ACT : Make a caterpillar using circles and colour it.

OVAL

Do you know what the shape of an egg is called? It is an OVAL. Sometimes, this shape is also called egg-shaped. Many balloons become oval in shape when you blow air into them. Rugby is played with an oval shaped ball.

ACT : Blow a balloon so that it takes an oval shape. Help the child to paste strips of paper dipped in water and glue solution and cover the balloon. Let it dry. Then, colour the strips and make them look like a dinosaur egg!

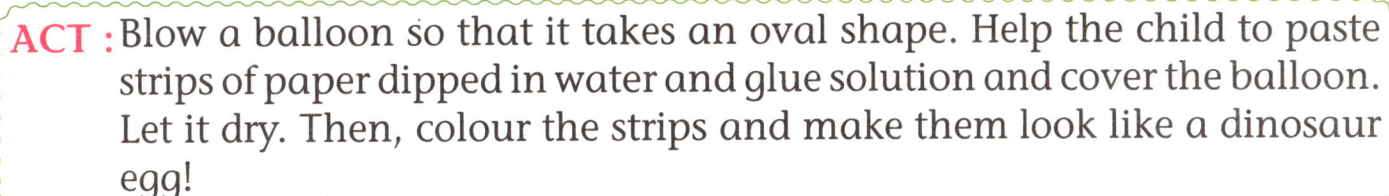

DIAMOND

Have you seen a kite? The shape of a kite is called DIAMOND. The diamond shape is also called a RHOMBUS. If you try and join two triangles, you will get a rhombus or a diamond shape.

ACT : Help the child to join two triangles and form a diamond. Ask the child to decorate the kites given below.

STAR

STAR shape is a big favourite among children. A star shape has five pointed corners. You must have looked at the stars in the sky. A starfish has five arms too. How many star shapes can you find in this picture?

HEXAGON

HEXAGON is a shape that has six corners. It is a rectangle with a triangle on top and one below it. A honey bee lives in a honeycomb that has the shape of a hexagon. Have you seen it?

ACT : Use six colours to colour the hexagons in the beehive.

CONE

CONE is a shape easy to recognise because you get ice cream in it. It looks like a hollow triangle. Birthday party caps are also shaped like big cones. You can even make paper cones and fill them with popcorn.

ACT : Fill the ice cream cones with your favourite scoops!

Now, let us learn to count.

1 round and big Sun

2 tiny feet to help you run

3 big oval balloons filled with air

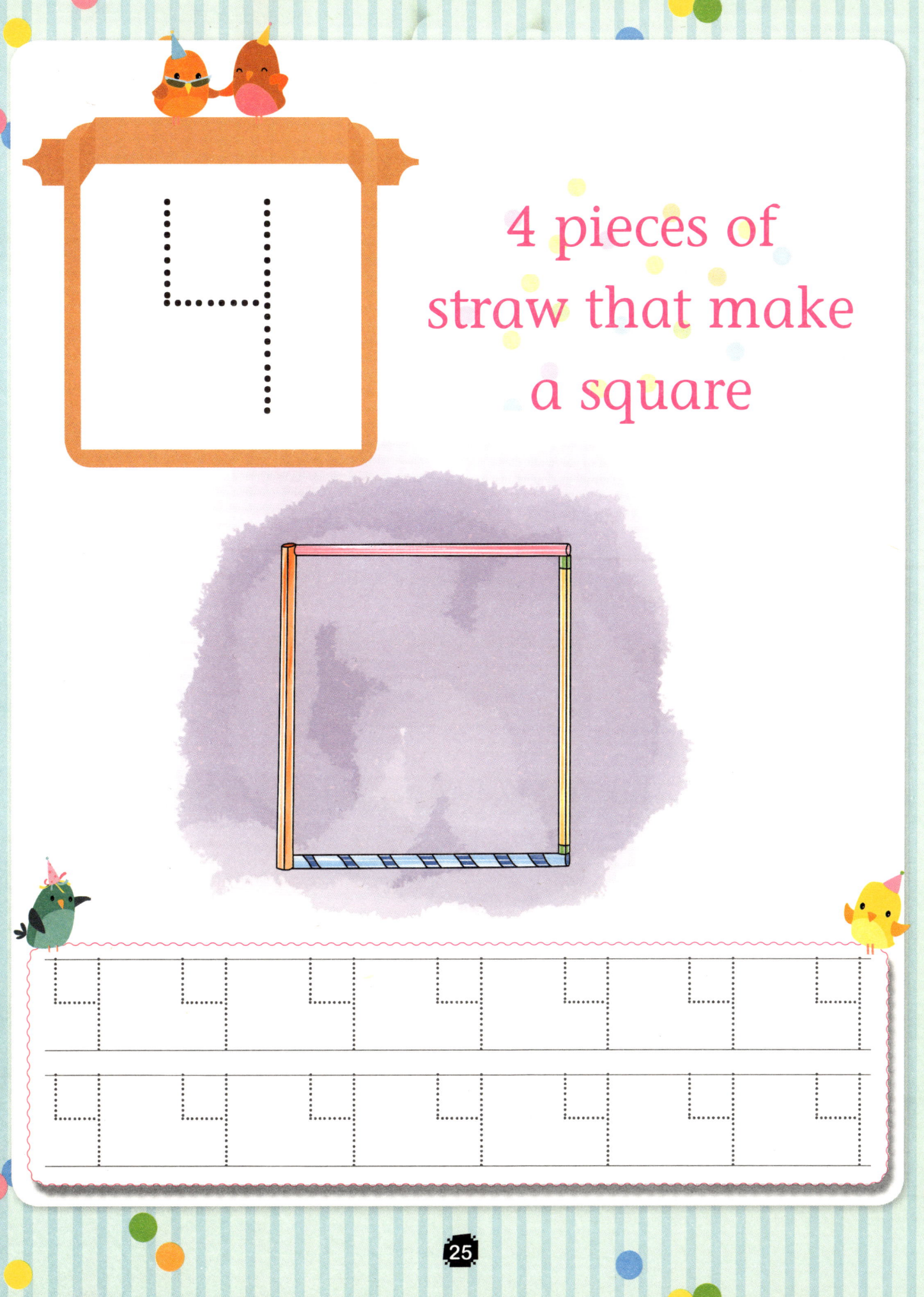

4 pieces of straw that make a square

5 are the corners of a star

6 yellow chicks sitting on my car

7 scoops of ice cream in a cone

8 pretty houses made of stone

9 cookies on my plate to eat

Let us learn............

One big sun that is round

Two little feet to run on the ground

Three oval balloons filled with air

Four long straws make a square

Five pointed corners to my star

Six yellow chicks sitting on my car

Seven scoops of ice cream in a cone

Eight pretty houses made of stone

Nine cookies on my plate to eat

Ten little fingers to print on a sheet!